MERMAID COLORING BOOK FOR ADULTS & KIDS

— RUSS FOCUS —

ISBN-13: 978-1725192997   ISBN-10: 1725192993

PUBLISHED BY RUSS FOCUS COPYRIGHT © 2018 ALL RIGHTS RESERVED
NO PART OF THIS PUBLICATION MAY BE REPRODUCED IN ANY
FORM OR BY ANY MEANS WITHOUT WRITTEN PERMISSION OF THE PUBLISHER.
WE ARE NOT RESPONSIBLE FOR UNSOLICITES MATERIAL PUBLISHED IN USA

www.russfocus.com

www.ingramcontent.com/pod-product-compliance
Lightning Source LLC
Chambersburg PA
CBHW062334220526
45469CB00008B/2713